EXPLORING OUR OCEANS

NUDIBRANCH

SUSAN H. GRAY

Published in the United States of America by Cherry Lake Publishing
Ann Arbor, Michigan
www.cherrylakepublishing.com

Consultants: Dominique A. Didier, PhD, Associate Professor, Department of Biology, Millersville University; Marla Conn, ReadAbility, Inc.
Book design: Sleeping Bear Press

Photo Credits: ©Kerry Werry/Thinkstock, cover, 1, 13; ©James van den Broek/Shutterstock Images, 5, 25; ©worldswildlifewonders/Shutterstock Images, 7; ©Khoroshunova Olga/Shutterstock Images, 9; ©Dorling Kindersley/Thinkstock, 10; ©scubaluna/Shutterstock Images, 15; ©orlandin/Shutterstock Images, 16; ©Joe Belanger/Shutterstock Images, 17; ©Izanbar/Dreamstime.com, 19; ©Robert Daniels/Dreamstime.com, 21; ©Ye Choh Wah/Shutterstock Images, 22; ©Arnon Polin/Shutterstock Images, 23, 26; ©Dray van Beeck/Shutterstock Images, 27; ©Marjan Visser Photography/Shutterstock Images, 29

Library of Congress Cataloging-in-Publication Data

Gray, Susan Heinrichs, author.
Nudibranch / by Susan H. Gray.
pages cm. — (Exploring our oceans)
Summary: "Discover facts about nudibranchs, including physical features, habitat, life cycle, food, and threats to these ocean creatures. Photos, captions, and keywords supplement the narrative of this informational text"—Provided by publisher.
Audience: Age 8-12.
Audience: Grades 4 to 6.
Includes bibliographical references and index.
ISBN 978-1-63188-021-6 (hardcover)—ISBN 978-1-63188-064-3 (pbk.)— ISBN 978-1-63188-107-7 (pdf)—
ISBN 978-1-63188-150-3 (ebook) 1. Nudibranchia—Juvenile literature. [1. Sea slugs.] I. Title. II. Title: Nudibranch.
III. Series: 21st century skills library. Exploring our oceans.

QL430.4.G73 2014
594.3—dc23 2014005352

Cherry Lake Publishing would like to acknowledge the work of The Partnership for 21st Century Skills. Please visit *www.p21.org* for more information.

Printed in the United States of America
Corporate Graphics Inc.

ABOUT THE AUTHOR

Susan H. Gray has a master's degree in zoology. She has worked in research and has taught college-level science classes. Susan has also written more than 140 science and reference books, but especially likes to write about animals. She and her husband, Michael, live in Cabot, Arkansas.

TABLE OF CONTENTS

GAG!

A hungry fish slipped quietly around the reef, hunting for an easy meal. Suddenly, he spied the perfect snack. Creeping along the seafloor was an orange, slow-moving, juicy-looking animal. This would be too easy. The fish zoomed toward the animal and took a bite out of its side. Immediately the fish stopped swimming. Its body jerked as it spit orange tissue into the water. That animal tasted awful! The fish paused, then shot away. He would never make that mistake again!

This colorful nudibranch might catch the eye of hungry animals, but it tastes horrible.

The fish had just tried his first taste of a nudibranch. Nudibranchs are soft-bodied animals that are related to slugs and snails. In fact, many people call them sea slugs. They live in every one of the world's oceans. But they are especially common in warm waters. Many nudibranch **species** live on coral reefs where food is plentiful. Others prefer rocky or sandy areas.

People sometimes see nudibranchs in pools along rocky shores. When the tide rises, the rocks become covered with water. When the water **recedes**, shallow pools are left behind. These are called tide pools. They may be filled with small animals, including nudibranchs.

Most nudibranchs creep quietly around coral reefs or among rocks in shallow areas. In areas with strong currents, they flatten their bodies to avoid being washed away. A few nudibranchs, such as the Spanish shawl, are graceful swimmers in the open water.

Unlike most nudibranchs, the Spanish shawl can swim quite well.

LOOK AGAIN

LOOK CLOSELY AT THIS PHOTOGRAPH. HOW DO YOU THINK THE SPANISH SHAWL GOT ITS NAME?

The Nudibranch Body

There are more than 3,000 different nudibranch species. Each one has a soft body with a flattened underside. That underside is basically a large, muscular foot. As the animal travels, its muscles ripple in waves. In creeping nudibranchs, the muscles lift the foot and drop it a little farther ahead. This slowly propels the sea slug forward. In swimming nudibranchs, waves of muscle activity send the animal up, down, or forward through the water.

Nudibranchs have no legs to help them walk, so they must travel a different way.

BODY DIAGRAM

Nudibranchs have very simple bodies.

The blue sea slug is a tiny nudibranch that has a unique way of traveling. It swallows a gulp of air and holds it inside. This air bubble helps the animal float near the ocean's surface.

On the nudibranch's head is a pair of fingerlike organs called rhinophores. They serve as the animal's nose and taste buds. They pick up smells and tastes in the environment. When disturbed, the rhinophores draw down into protective pockets.

Many nudibranchs also have **tentacles** on their heads. They help the sea slugs feel their way as they creep. The animals have tiny eyes. These do not help them see clearly. Instead, they detect only light and shadows.

The mouth is on the underside of the head. It contains a rough organ called the **radula**. As the nudibranch glides over prey, the radula scrapes the prey's tissues. It then shreds them into tiny bits for eating.

Like other ocean animals, nudibranchs need special organs for breathing. These organs must be able to draw oxygen from the water and move it into the nudibranch's body. They must also force out waste gases. Some nudibranchs have fingerlike breathing structures covering their bodies. These are called **cerata**. Oxygen and waste gases pass right through them. Other nudibranchs breathe through gills. These are bushy or feathery structures, usually rising from the back.

The word *nudibranch* means "naked gills." This is a good name for these animals. Their gills and cerata are out in the open, unprotected.

THINK ABOUT IT

EVERY YEAR, SCIENTISTS DISCOVER NEW SPECIES OF NUDIBRANCHS. WHY HAVEN'T ALL THE SPECIES BEEN DISCOVERED BY NOW?

The cerata on the nudibranch help it to breathe.

NUDI-FOOD

Nudibranchs are **carnivores**. They feed on sea anemones, corals, jellyfish, **hydroids**, and sponges. They even eat other nudibranchs!

In some species, the radula is a ribbon with one or two rows of hooked teeth. In others, there may be many rows, or the teeth may be different sizes or shapes.

Some nudibranchs, such as the blue dragon, get something extra from their food. They graze on hydroids that contain algae in their bodies. When a nudibranch eats the hydroid, it takes in some of the algae, too. The algae stay in the nudibranch's body. Algae produce food through **photosynthesis**. This process provides food for the nudibranch, too.

Algae provide food for this blue dragon.

This photograph shows a nudibranch's two rhinophores.

All animals need food for energy. But nudibranchs get much more than energy from their food. They get protection. How does this work?

It works in several different ways. Some nudibranchs get protective colors from their food. Some develop a very bad taste that **repels** their enemies. And some actually get **venom** from their prey.

The red sponge nudibranch feeds on red and orange sponges. Some of the sponge's **pigments** stay inside the nudibranch's body. They give the slug its color. As the nudibranch creeps around its prey, it is hard for predators to see. The nudibranch is **camouflaged**.

Predators pass right by and never bother it.

Some nudibranchs taste bad. As the nudibranchs chomp on their prey, they take in bad-tasting substances from their prey's bodies. These substances don't seem to bother the nudibranchs. In fact, the nudibranchs keep them in their own bodies. The chemicals then spread throughout their tissues. Hungry predators that

This nudibranch may have eaten an orange sponge recently.

bite into these nudibranchs are in for a nasty surprise.

The nudibranchs with cerata have the best trick of all. They eat sea anemones. These are animals with stinging cells on their tentacles. Nudibranchs swallow the stinging cells whole with no problem. In time, the stinging cells become stored in the nudibranchs' cerata. They stay there until a predator dares to attack. Then the cells spring open and the stinging threads fire right into the enemy.

Some nudibranchs live among coral.

LOOK AGAIN

LOOK CLOSELY AT THIS PHOTOGRAPH SHOWING A CORAL'S STINGING TENTACLES. WHY DO YOU THINK THESE STINGING CELLS DON'T FIRE ON THE NUDIBRANCHS?

A Nudibranch's Life

Every nudibranch starts its life inside an egg. Adults lay hundreds or even thousands of eggs at once. They are massed together in clumps, strings, or ribbons. The strings or ribbons are usually crumpled or coiled. All of the eggs are held together by a jellylike material.

Adults do not tend to their eggs. However, they do not leave them unprotected. The jelly provides some safety. But the egg ribbons of the Spanish dancer also contain a nasty chemical. The chemical repels predators and keeps the eggs safe.

As hatching time gets closer, the baby nudibranchs do something interesting. They begin to spin in place. They do this while still inside the egg mass. Scientists think this may help to move nutrients and gases around. Spinning helps the babies get the materials they need to develop.

Nudibranch eggs are protected by a chemical that keeps predators away.

These nudibranchs, which each have male and female parts, are mating.

All nudibranchs have a short life span. Most species live less than a year. Some live less than a month. But before their time is up, they must grow up, mate, and lay eggs.

There are no male or female sea slugs. Instead, each animal has both male and female organs. Their male organs produce **sperm** cells, while the female organs produce eggs.

To mate, two members of the same species move next to each other. Each animal then deposits sperm cells into the body of the other one. The cells are stored there for a short time. Meanwhile, the eggs are developing elsewhere in their bodies. In time, the eggs unite with the sperm cells. Soon afterward, the adults lay down their egg masses.

Egg ribbons are coated in jelly for protection.

LOOK AGAIN

HERE IS A PHOTOGRAPH OF AN EGG MASS. WHY IS IT NECESSARY FOR A NUDIBRANCH TO LAY SO MANY EGGS?

EXPERTS AT SURVIVAL

How do the nudibranchs manage to survive? After all, they move slowly and cannot outrun their enemies. They have no shells to draw into for safety. Their bodies are soft and can be easily damaged. They have terrible eyesight. And their delicate breathing organs are hanging outside of their bodies! Why haven't these delicate fragile animals died out?

The nudibranchs survive because they are masters of defense. They use every trick available to scare, poison, distract, hide from, and escape their enemies.

Those that taste bad are not likely to be eaten by predators. And predators definitely avoid the ones with stinging cells.

This nudibranch looks like a yummy snack, but it is probably poisonous.

Sometimes nudibranchs are the same colors as their surroundings.

The sea slugs with dull colors are able to hide in plain sight. They just blend in with their sandy or muddy surroundings. Those with shocking colors warn predators to stay away. If a fish nips at a colorful but terrible-tasting nudibranch, he will remember those colors. He is not likely to taste a nudibranch again.

The nudibranchs with cerata have one more trick. They know how to distract their enemies. When they sense danger, they just drop a few cerata from their bodies. The cerata wiggle around on their own, drawing attention away from the nudibranch itself.

A predator would not be interested in this bold-colored nudibranch.

Despite all of their safety features, nudibranchs can't escape every danger. Sea spiders, sea worms, and some crabs eat them. Worse yet, in some areas their food supply is dwindling.

The corals they eat are dying because of changes in the environment. Animals living around coral reefs are also dying. If nudibranchs can't find enough corals or anemones to eat, they will be in trouble, too.

Many experts are looking into this problem. They hope to protect the corals, anemones, nudibranchs, and other reef animals. Everyone wants these beautiful creatures around for years to come.

GO DEEPER

REREAD THE TEXT ABOUT THE ANIMALS THAT DO EAT NUDIBRANCHS. WHY DO YOU THINK THEY AREN'T BOTHERED BY THE BAD TASTE OR THE STINGING CELLS?

Nudibranchs exist in a large variety of colors.

THINK ABOUT IT

- In chapter 1, we learned about animals found in tide pools. Why do you think living in a tide pool would be dangerous to some animals?
- Sea slugs produce a trail of slime just like land slugs do. What are some reasons to lay down a slime trail?
- Many sea slugs have dazzling colors to keep predators away. Can you think of other animals that use bright colors to warn predators?

LEARN MORE

FURTHER READING

MacQuitty, Miranda. *Ocean.* New York: DK Publishing, 2008.

Parker, Steve. *Ocean and Sea.* New York: Scholastic, 2012.

Spelman, Lucy. *Animal Encyclopedia: 2,500 Animals with Photos, Maps, and More!* Washington, DC: National Geographic Children's Books, 2012.

WEB SITES

Little Animals: Big Bag of Tricks
http://aquarium.ucsd.edu/Education/Learning_Resources/Voyager_for_Kids/nudibranch/index.html
This Web site provides information about a nudibranch's senses and how it survives.

National Geographic Kids—Nudibranchs
http://kids.nationalgeographic.com/kids/photos/gallery/nudibranchs
View colorful photographs and read interesting facts about many types of nudibranchs.

GLOSSARY

camouflaged (KAM-uh-flahjd) when an animal's natural coloring enables it to blend in with its surroundings

carnivores (KAHR-nuh-vorz) animals that eat other animals

cerata (KER-ah-tuh) fingerlike breathing structures covering a nudibranch's body

hydroids (HYE-droidz) small, simple, soft-bodied animals with tentacles

photosynthesis (fot-toh-SIN-thi-sis) the process of using light energy to combine air and water to make a plant's food

pigments (PIG-muhnts) substances that give plants or animals their color

radula (RA-juh-luh) a tonguelike structure with raspy teeth used for scraping food particles off a surface and drawing them into the mouth

recedes (rih-SEEDZ) goes or moves away

repels (rih-PELZ) drives or forces something away

species (SPEE-sheez) one type, or kind, of plant or animal

sperm (SPURM) male reproductive cell

tentacles (TEN-tuh-kuhlz) slender, flexible limbs or appendages in an animal, used for grasping or moving around, or containing sense organs

venom (VEN-uhm) a poisonous fluid that some animals secrete and inject into their prey

INDEX